Once upon a time, in the depths c̶ ̶ ̶
Lived a tiny little village; a villag
Placed on the tip of a pretty pur
Lived this bug village, sunshine c
The village was full with a variet, ̶ ̶ ̶ ̶insects.
Of course, this included the usual suspects:

Grasshoppers and ground beetles; earwigs and earthworms,
Honey bees and house ants; spider and silkworms.
They were fat ones, and nice ones, and some with a spot.
Funny ones, and small ones, and some who sneezed a lot.
But our story begins with one special insect,
Niko, the bug who learned to deal with disrespect.

1

My differences are great, and I smile with glee.
I'm special my parents said. I'm the only me!

Niko, they call me. That is my name.
Instead of two antennas;
with one is how I came.

This makes me quite different as I'm sure you'll recognize. But I like who I am I've come to realize.

As I prepared for the first day of school.
I was nervous and excited and wanted to look cool.
So, I gathered my supplies and zipped up my backpack.

I packed up my lunch and grabbed a good snack.
The thought of my difference didn't cross my mind.
This all changed when I met the bully of all kind.

On the first day of school, as the caterpillar bus arrived;
Mom kissed my one antenna and said her goodbyes.

I looked around nervously to find a good seat,
Hoping to find a friend who's interesting, intelligent, and neat.
But instead all I heard was a growing loud mumble,
As the meanest bug of all started to rumble.

"Look! Look at that bug! Hey, what is your name?"
"Niko." I whispered and immediately felt shame.
"Well, where did your other antenna go?"

Suddenly, my worst fear of all quickly came true,
As the other bugs on the bus joined in with him too.
I quietly slid into the very back seat,
Hoping this day would be quickly complete.

I couldn't understand why they thought I was strange.
Sure, I have differences; but, we all have things we would change.
The bus finally stopped, after what seemed like forever,
This was not going well for a first day endeavor.
I slowly slumped off, dragging my feet,
Hoping for the end of this horrible defeat.

Later that night as I tried to go to bed,
horrible thoughts kept running through my head.

I always thought I was just plain-old, cool, Niko.
I was so mad at myself; I felt I could scream!
I had never hated myself; until the bully bug, Whufflecheem.

The next day, I bravely entered class and quickly took my seat.
I was bold, confident, with a mindset that couldn't be beat.
But then a little bug yelled...

My bravery slipped away and was replaced with great fear!
What more could Whufflecheem want with me?
Oh dear! Oh dear!

Whufflecheem is not your ordinary bug bully.
He's mean, calls you names, and makes you hate yourself fully.
The other bugs in the school have a song that they sing…

All the school bugs and teachers gathered around,
Near the big tree on our lily-pad playground.
Whufflecheem stomped up, and I stifled a scream.
An intimidating look from his ghastly face gleamed.

His words shocked me making me question, he says differences are bad, yet we all have some. It is true Whufflecheem said some very hurtful things.

Of course, I could shoot back, and take my own swings. After all, Whufflecheem deserves to be taught, But the choice is mine, so I stood there and thought.

All the bugs waited, as Whufflecheem glared, But I couldn't be persuaded, and I wouldn't be scared. The choice is mine and soon you will see, the type of bug I chose to be.

What should I do? Should I...

Walk away?
Turn to page 13

Talk it out?
Turn to page 18

Fight back?
Turn to page 27

Walking away is what I thought best.
Others may disagree, but this is not their test.
Sure, I could talk back making Whufflecheem feel small,
But what will be gained from all that after all?

I CHOOSE TO WALK AWAY

Whufflecheem was awful, horrible, and rude.
I never want to be compared to that type of dude.
So, I swallowed my ego and tackled by pride.
Turned on my heels, and started my stride.
I walked away quickly, but very quite sure,
I choose the right path. It is much more mature.

Of course, Whufflecheem has his own thoughts about this.
He came here to fight, he began to yell with a hiss.
I ignored every scream, every loud shout,
And with each new step, my mind cleared of doubt.

"Niko the Freako!" he began to chant.
He called me mean names and continued his rant.
But I didn't care a bit; no not anymore.
He'll say what he'll say, but I've settled the score.

Walking away may seem like a small gesture,
But really, it's more when you see the big picture.
Walking away was not simple to do.
It took courage, and patience, and a lot of attitude.

You see, by choosing to walk away, The control and fear melted away.

Whufflecheem's thoughts and mean words no longer mattered. He'll always be a bully, but I will be better.

Of course, that isn't the end of it all,
Whufflecheem tried to restart the brawl.
The name calling got worse, and he glared at me often.
Being stopped in a hall or tripped was quite common.

But every time he tried to bother me,
I'd get back up and walk away swiftly.
Eventually the bullying came to an end,
He was the one left without a friend.
The other bugs at school watched me walk away.
They agreed this was best and invited me to play.
We all ignored Whufflecheem each day and each night,
He eventually decided to finally give up his fight.

I am proud of myself for walking away.
I wouldn't change a thing of that very brave day.
I chose to take the path of peace,
And from that moment on, I found my bullying release.

Let's talk, I thought. Confront the issue head on.
Let's deal with the meanness and let it be gone.
Yes, using our words and talking was best.
Others may disagree, but this is not their test.

I said to Wufflecheem, confident and strong...Tell me, why do you bully me and treat me so wrong?

I've never hurt you, or kicked you, or stomped on your toe. So why tease me and bother me? Please, I must know!

I CHOOSE TO TALK IT OUT

Whufflecheem glared at me with a gleam of pure hate.
I stood there and thought... Well, this should be great.

He's gonna give it to me;
I just know that he will.
He'll tear me to pieces, then go
for the kill. He'll point out all my
flaws, again and again,
for all the other bugs to see
and join in.

This is what will
happen. I know
it for a fact.
Oh, I should have
kept quiet and just
let him attack.

As I stood there and waited for the ultimate blow,
Something different happened; something started to show.

No, it wasn't hate I saw on his face anymore,
Instead there was kindness, niceness and something more.
Whufflecheem twiddled his antennas and looked down at his feet,
And meekly whispered "Would you like to have a seat?"
He pointed toward two mushrooms hidden by a tree.

I cautiously followed him waiting for the attack,
But it never came, instead, he offered a snack.
As we nibbled on our leaves, I let him just speak.
He began by simply saying, "You aren't a freak."
My eyes became huge as I stared at him in shock.
Was he actually being nice? Or was this just talk?

Whufflecheem went on. He wanted to explain.
I sat there and listened, it was clear he felt pain.

It's true you are different and I don't like that much. But it's not why you think, there is still much more stuff.

You are small and weak, and look a silly color. You are nerdy, and weird, and as light as a feather. But these aren't the reasons I hate you the most. I hate that you're happy, and I'm not, not even close.

His words amazed me, and I was slightly offended,
But I thought I'd let that go; something bigger has ended.

Whufflecheem kept talking on and on,
Explaining his life and all he'd done wrong.

I have differences as well, just as all bugs do, But mine make me feel worse; far worse than yours do. I don't like myself much or the mean things I have done.

I pretend I don't care and keep moving on. I don't tell anyone or let them close enough to know, so, meanness and rudeness are all that I show. I have treated you poorly, and this is not right. I am sorry for bullying you. I don't want to fight.

"Thank you." I said and I meant it so fully,
This is all I ever wanted from this big bug bully.
I accepted his apology, but had something to say.
He needed to know the consequence of acting this way.

He nodded his head and shook my bug hand,
We had agreed; the bullying is banned.
By using our words and talking it out,
I was able to learn what the bullying was about.

Whufflecheem presents a horrible exterior,
But inside he is hurting; now that is much clearer.
We are not the best of friends, but we get along splendid,
It's amazing what can change when a conflict is mended.

Just then, a great thought crossed my mind,
He thinks he's so big, well I too can be unkind.
This guy can't talk to me like that and make me look dumb,
I'll show him. I'll shoot right back. I'll tell him he's scum.
I'm not going to be intimidated one second more.
He wants to fight? Fine, I'll knock him to the floor.
My eyes became mean, and I growled a fierce growl.
"Come get me!" I screamed and started to prowl.
I stomped right up to him, looked him straight in the face.
"Let's do this! I'm here! I'm ready! Let's cut to the chase!"

Whufflecheem, of course, will not back down.
He puckers his lips and frowns a great frown.
His blazing eyes pierced right through my soul.
He is trying to scare me; his ultimate goal.
We stand there a moment each trying to decide,
What happens next? Do we fight, or do we hide?

I really dislike this Wufflecheem bug!
He thinks he's so smart with his face looking smug.

I'll tell you what Whufflecheem, you think you're so great? You're nothing but a coward; a trait that I hate! You pick on those who are different and small, yet you yourself, are starting to stall.

You aren't so big, strong, or smart. You're teeny and tiny, and don't have a heart. I could never treat bugs the way that you do, But that's why other's like me, and no one likes you!

My words make Whufflecheem madder than mad.
He swings at my face, and might I just add,
He might have hit me if I were not so petite.
As his fist swooshed over my head, he landed in the street.

I pointed my finger and I laughed out loud.
Then I noticed a parting throughout the bug crowd.
It was principal Boll Weevil and he didn't look happy.
He shouted "Get over here right now! Make it quite snappy!"
We both jumped to our feet and ran to his side;
I quickly realized being nice, I should have tried.

Straight to his office, he took us inside,
He told us to sit and glared at us wide.
"Just what is this all about, the fighting and yelling?"
"You two should know better, so you need to start telling."
I am too embarrassed to speak a single word;
I simply look down while my punishment was heard.
Three days' detention is what we both got,
"What will my parents think?" is all that I thought.

I am now the same as Whufflecheem; a big old bully, I have become the thing that I hated most fully. The punishment isn't what matters to me; It's what I am, and what others will see. The lesson I learned I'll gladly share with you, be careful of how you act and the things you do. Once you raise your fist or call someone a slug, the tables will turn, and you'll be the Bully Bug.

30480320R00021

Made in the USA
Lexington, KY
09 February 2019